Der Unartige Roboter: Zweisprachige Englisch-Deutsche Geschichten

My Pommeline

Published by My Pommeline, 2024.

DER UNARTIGE ROBOTER: ZWEISPRACHIGE ENGLISCH-DEUTSCHE GESCHICHTEN

First edition. October 15, 2024.

Copyright © 2024 My Pommeline.

ISBN: 979-8224049745

Written by My Pommeline.

Table of Contents

Aunt Mildred's Magic Biscuit Tin

In the quaint village of Maplewood, where the sun shone brightly and birds sang sweet melodies, there lived a plucky girl named Sophie. Sophie loved two things above all else: her pet rabbit, Mr. Flopsy, and visiting her eccentric Aunt Mildred. Aunt Mildred was known far and wide for her incredible baking skills, especially her legendary biscuits. But what made Aunt Mildred's biscuits truly special was her mysterious tin.

The Mysterious Biscuit Tin

One rainy afternoon, Sophie was visiting Aunt Mildred's cozy cottage. The air was filled with the delicious aroma of freshly baked goods, and Sophie's tummy rumbled in excitement.

As they sat at the kitchen table, Sophie spotted the old biscuit tin in the corner. It was an ornate, antique tin adorned with swirls of gold and intricate floral designs.

"Aunt Mildred, can I have a biscuit?" Sophie asked, pointing to the tin.

"Ah, but those are no ordinary biscuits!" Aunt Mildred exclaimed, her eyes twinkling mischievously. "They are magic biscuits. Each one grants a temporary superpower to whoever eats it."

Sophie's eyes widened in disbelief. "Magic biscuits? Really?"

"Indeed!" Aunt Mildred chuckled. "But be warned: the powers only last for one hour, and you never know what you might get!"

The First Biscuit

Curiosity bubbled inside Sophie. "Can I try one?"

"Of course, my dear! But choose wisely!" Aunt Mildred said, handing her the biscuit tin.

Sophie opened the tin and peered inside. The biscuits were shaped like stars, moons, and little animals, each one more tempting than the last. She selected a star-shaped biscuit, its surface sparkling with a hint of magic.

With a quick bite, she felt a strange tingle run through her body. Suddenly, she noticed something incredible: she could hear the thoughts of Mr. Flopsy, who was munching on a carrot nearby!

"I can talk to you, Sophie!" he squeaked excitedly. "I've always wanted to tell you that I think carrots are the best thing ever!"

Sophie laughed, her heart bursting with joy. "This is amazing, Mr. Flopsy! What else do you want to say?"

"Can we have more carrots?" he replied earnestly.

Just then, the hour was up, and the magical connection faded. Mr. Flopsy returned to munching silently, but Sophie's smile lingered. "That was so much fun!"

The Superpower Parade

Excited by her experience, Sophie turned to Aunt Mildred. "Can I try another one?"

"Absolutely!" Aunt Mildred replied, grinning.

Sophie reached into the tin again, this time picking out a moon-shaped biscuit. She took a bite, and this time, she felt a powerful rush. Suddenly, she found herself levitating off the ground!

"Look, Aunt Mildred! I'm flying!" Sophie squealed, zooming around the kitchen, nearly touching the ceiling.

"Careful, dear!" Aunt Mildred laughed, her eyes gleaming with delight. "Just remember, it only lasts for an hour!"

Sophie floated around the room, giggling and twirling, until the magic faded and she gently floated back down to the floor.

"What's next?" Sophie asked, her eyes sparkling with excitement.

The Biscuit Challenge

Determined to explore all the biscuit's possibilities, Sophie and Aunt Mildred decided to organize a *Biscuit Challenge*. They invited all the children in the village to try a magic biscuit and see what superpower they could get.

The next day, children filled Aunt Mildred's garden, buzzing with anticipation. Each child chose a biscuit, and soon the garden was filled with laughter and shouts of joy.

"I can run faster than the wind!" shouted Sam, racing in circles around the garden.

"I can turn invisible!" squealed Lily, disappearing and reappearing behind a tree.

"Watch me! I can jump higher than a house!" exclaimed Ben, leaping into the air.

Sophie felt a warm glow of happiness watching her friends experience the magic. Each biscuit brought laughter and excitement, creating memories that would last a lifetime.

The Final Biscuit

As the sun began to set, Sophie realized it was time for one last biscuit. She wanted to try something truly special.

"What should I pick?" she wondered aloud, staring at the remaining biscuits.

Aunt Mildred smiled knowingly. "Perhaps try the biscuit shaped like a heart."

With a sense of adventure, Sophie grabbed the heart-shaped biscuit. Taking a big bite, she felt a surge of warmth. Suddenly, she found herself surrounded by a glowing light, and before she knew it, she had the power to spread joy!

Sophie raced around the garden, and with every hug and high-five she gave, her friends lit up with laughter and happiness. It was as if the whole village was glowing with joy!

The Power of Magic and Friendship

As the magic faded, Sophie gathered her friends for a final hug, feeling grateful for the day they had shared.

"Thank you, Aunt Mildred! This was the best day ever!" she exclaimed.

Aunt Mildred chuckled, "Remember, Sophie, the true magic comes from the joy and love we share with others, not just the biscuits."

With her heart full of happiness, Sophie realized that the best superpower of all was the ability to bring friends together and spread joy. As the children returned home, she made a promise to Aunt Mildred: they would continue to share the magic of biscuits and friendship for many years to come.

And so, the legend of Aunt Mildred's magic biscuit tin grew, bringing joy, laughter, and a little bit of magic to Maplewood, one biscuit at a time.

Aunt Mildreds magische Keksdose

Im malerischen Dorf Maplewood, wo die Sonne hell schien und die Vögel süße Melodien sangen, lebte ein mutiges Mädchen namens Sophie. Sophie liebte zwei Dinge über alles: ihren Hasen Mr. Flopsy und den Besuch bei ihrer exzentrischen Tante Mildred. Tante Mildred war weit und breit für ihre unglaublichen Backkünste bekannt, besonders für ihre legendären Kekse. Aber was Tante Mildreds Kekse wirklich besonders machte, war ihre mysteriöse Keksdose.

Die geheimnisvolle Keksdose

Eines regnerischen Nachmittags besuchte Sophie Tante Mildreds gemütliches Häuschen. Der Duft von frisch gebackenen Leckereien erfüllte die Luft, und Sophies Magen knurrte vor Vorfreude.

Als sie am Küchentisch saßen, entdeckte Sophie die alte Keksdose in der Ecke. Es war eine verzierte, antike Dose, geschmückt mit goldenen Wirbeln und filigranen Blumenmustern.

„Tante Mildred, kann ich einen Keks haben?" fragte Sophie und zeigte auf die Dose.

„Ah, aber das sind keine gewöhnlichen Kekse!" rief Tante Mildred aus, ihre Augen blitzten verschmitzt. „Das sind magische Kekse. Jeder verleiht demjenigen, der ihn isst, eine vorübergehende Superkraft."

Sophies Augen weiteten sich ungläubig. „Magische Kekse? Wirklich?"

„In der Tat!" kicherte Tante Mildred. „Aber sei gewarnt: Die Kräfte halten nur eine Stunde, und du weißt nie, welche du bekommst!"

Der erste Keks

Neugierde blubberte in Sophie auf. „Darf ich einen probieren?"

„Natürlich, mein Schatz! Aber wähle weise!" sagte Tante Mildred und reichte ihr die Keksdose.

Sophie öffnete die Dose und spähte hinein. Die Kekse hatten die Form von Sternen, Monden und kleinen Tieren, jeder sah verlockender aus als der andere. Sie wählte einen sternförmigen Keks, dessen Oberfläche mit einem Hauch Magie funkelte.

Mit einem schnellen Biss spürte sie ein seltsames Kribbeln durch ihren Körper laufen. Plötzlich bemerkte sie etwas Unglaubliches: Sie konnte die Gedanken von Mr. Flopsy hören, der in der Nähe an einer Karotte knabberte!

„Ich kann mit dir sprechen, Sophie!" quietschte er aufgeregt. „Ich wollte dir schon immer sagen, dass ich Karotten für das Beste überhaupt halte!"

Sophie lachte, ihr Herz war voller Freude. „Das ist fantastisch, Mr. Flopsy! Was möchtest du noch sagen?"

„Können wir mehr Karotten haben?" antwortete er ernsthaft.

Gerade in diesem Moment war die Stunde um, und die magische Verbindung verblasste. Mr. Flopsy knabberte wieder still vor sich hin, aber Sophies Lächeln blieb. „Das hat so viel Spaß gemacht!"

Die Superkräfte-Parade

Begeistert von ihrer Erfahrung wandte sich Sophie an Tante Mildred. „Darf ich noch einen probieren?"

„Aber natürlich!" antwortete Tante Mildred grinsend.

Sophie griff wieder in die Dose, dieses Mal wählte sie einen mondförmigen Keks. Sie nahm einen Bissen, und sofort spürte sie einen mächtigen Energieschub. Plötzlich schwebte sie über dem Boden!

„Schau, Tante Mildred! Ich fliege!" rief Sophie und sauste durch die Küche, fast die Decke berührend.

„Vorsichtig, mein Kind!" lachte Tante Mildred, ihre Augen glänzten vor Freude. „Denk daran, es hält nur eine Stunde!"

Sophie schwebte lachend und wirbelnd durch den Raum, bis die Magie nachließ und sie sanft auf den Boden zurückkehrte.

„Was kommt als Nächstes?" fragte Sophie, ihre Augen funkelten vor Aufregung.

Die Keks-Challenge

Entschlossen, alle Möglichkeiten der Kekse zu erkunden, beschlossen Sophie und Tante Mildred, eine Keks-Challenge zu organisieren. Sie luden alle Kinder aus dem Dorf ein, einen magischen Keks zu probieren und zu sehen, welche Superkraft sie bekamen.

Am nächsten Tag füllten Kinder Tante Mildreds Garten, aufgeregt vor Vorfreude. Jedes Kind wählte einen Keks, und bald war der Garten erfüllt von Lachen und Freudenschreien.

„Ich kann schneller als der Wind rennen!" rief Sam, der in Kreisen um den Garten rannte.

„Ich kann unsichtbar werden!" quietschte Lily, die hinter einem Baum verschwand und wieder auftauchte.

„Seht mich an! Ich kann höher als ein Haus springen!" rief Ben und sprang in die Luft.

Sophie spürte ein warmes Glücksgefühl, als sie ihren Freunden dabei zusah, die Magie zu erleben. Jeder Keks brachte Lachen und Aufregung, und sie schufen Erinnerungen, die ein Leben lang halten würden.

Der letzte Keks

Als die Sonne begann unterzugehen, wurde Sophie klar, dass es Zeit für den letzten Keks war. Sie wollte etwas ganz Besonderes ausprobieren.

„Welchen soll ich nehmen?" fragte sie laut und starrte auf die restlichen Kekse.

Tante Mildred lächelte wissend. „Vielleicht probierst du den Keks in Herzform."

Mit einem Gefühl von Abenteuer griff Sophie nach dem herzförmigen Keks. Mit einem großen Bissen spürte sie eine Welle von Wärme. Plötzlich war sie von einem leuchtenden Licht umgeben, und bevor sie es wusste, hatte sie die Kraft, Freude zu verbreiten!

Sophie rannte durch den Garten, und mit jeder Umarmung und jedem High-Five, das sie verteilte, strahlten ihre Freunde vor Lachen und Glück. Es war, als ob das ganze Dorf vor Freude erstrahlte!

Die Kraft der Magie und der Freundschaft

Als die Magie nachließ, versammelte Sophie ihre Freunde zu einer letzten Umarmung, dankbar für den Tag, den sie gemeinsam erlebt hatten.

„Danke, Tante Mildred! Das war der beste Tag aller Zeiten!" rief sie aus.

Tante Mildred kicherte: „Denk daran, Sophie, die wahre Magie kommt von der Freude und Liebe, die wir miteinander teilen, nicht nur von den Keksen."

Mit einem Herz voller Glück erkannte Sophie, dass die beste Superkraft von allen die Fähigkeit war, Freunde zusammenzubringen und Freude zu verbreiten. Als die Kinder nach Hause gingen, versprach sie Tante Mildred, dass sie die Magie der Kekse und der Freundschaft noch viele Jahre teilen würden.

Und so wuchs die Legende von Tante Mildreds magischer Keksdose weiter, brachte Freude, Lachen und ein kleines bisschen Magie nach Maplewood – Keks für Keks.

The Day the School Bus Flew

In the bustling town of Whimsyville, where the skies were always blue and adventure lurked around every corner, there was a school bus named Buzzy. Buzzy was no ordinary bus; he was bright yellow with a happy face painted on the front and a cheerful horn that sounded like a giggle. The kids loved Buzzy, but little did they know that he had a secret—Buzzy could fly!

The Magical Morning

One bright morning, as the students piled onto Buzzy for their regular school day, a strange shimmer enveloped the bus. The children chatted excitedly, oblivious to the twinkling magic filling the air. Little did they know that today would be anything but ordinary.

"Good morning, Buzzy!" shouted Emma, the class president, as she took her seat beside her best friend, Leo. "Are you ready for another day of school?"

Buzzy honked cheerfully in response, but today, he felt a little different. Today, he could sense the magic bubbling inside him.

As the bus rumbled down Maple Street, the usual route suddenly turned into a sparkling path of colorful lights. The children gasped as they noticed the scenery shifting outside the windows.

"Look! The trees are turning into candy canes!" Leo shouted, eyes wide with wonder.

Suddenly, Buzzy took a deep breath and, with a joyful roar, lifted off the ground! The kids screamed in delight, their hearts racing with excitement.

"Hold on tight, everyone!" Buzzy announced in a cheerful voice. "We're going on a flying adventure!"

The Adventure Begins

The bus soared higher and higher, leaving Whimsyville behind. The children gazed out of the windows, watching their town shrink below them.

"Where are we going, Buzzy?" Emma asked, her excitement bubbling over.

"To the Land of Dreams!" Buzzy replied. "Where every child's imagination comes to life!"

As they flew over fluffy white clouds, Buzzy zigzagged through the air, twisting and turning like a roller coaster. The kids shrieked with joy as they passed through a rainbow, and each color splashed against their faces like a warm hug.

The Land of Dreams

Before they knew it, Buzzy landed softly in the Land of Dreams, a place where everything was vibrant and magical. The ground sparkled with glitter, and the trees were made of lollipops.

"Welcome to the Land of Dreams!" Buzzy exclaimed. "Time to explore!"

The kids burst out of the bus, their laughter echoing through the candy-colored landscape. They raced toward a gigantic chocolate fountain, where they dipped strawberries and marshmallows, giggling as chocolate dripped down their faces.

Suddenly, they heard a joyful sound. A group of playful unicorns pranced toward them, their manes shimmering in the sunlight.

"Hop on!" one of the unicorns said. "We'll take you on a ride!"

A Magical Ride

One by one, the children climbed onto the unicorns' backs, feeling the soft fur beneath them. The unicorns galloped through fields of flowers that sang sweet melodies, and the children laughed with pure joy.

"Look at that!" Leo pointed as they soared over a meadow where children were flying kites shaped like dragons. "This is the best day ever!"

As they rode, Buzzy watched from the side, beaming with happiness at the joy he had brought to his friends.

After a wonderful hour filled with laughter and exploration, Buzzy called out, "Time to go, kids! There's more adventure waiting for us!"

The Magical World Tour

With a cheerful honk, Buzzy took to the skies again, soaring over mountains that sparkled with jewels and lakes that glimmered like diamonds.

"Now we're heading to the Jungle of Giggles!" Buzzy announced as they flew through a fluffy cloud shaped like a rabbit.

When they landed, the children were greeted by friendly animals that told jokes. A wise old owl hooted, "Why don't scientists trust atoms? Because they make up everything!" The kids erupted in laughter, their giggles ringing out like music.

"Next stop!" Buzzy said, lifting off once more. "The Land of Ice Cream!"

As they landed in a world where everything was made of ice cream, the kids jumped out, excited to taste flavors they had never imagined. They built ice cream castles and even had a snowball fight with frozen yogurt!

Homeward Bound

After what felt like a magical day of endless adventures, Buzzy said, "Alright, friends, it's time to head back to Whimsyville!"

With one last glance at the Land of Ice Cream, the children climbed aboard Buzzy, their hearts filled with memories of laughter and magic.

As Buzzy flew back, the sun began to set, painting the sky with shades of orange and pink.

"I never want this day to end!" Emma exclaimed, her heart brimming with happiness.

"Me neither!" the others agreed, their eyes sparkling with excitement.

The Landing

With a gentle landing, Buzzy touched down back at the school, the children still buzzing with joy.

"Thanks for the best adventure ever, Buzzy!" Leo said, giving the bus a pat.

"Anytime, friends! Remember, magic is everywhere if you know where to look," Buzzy replied with a wink.

As the children headed into the school, they couldn't stop talking about their flying adventure. They promised to share the story with everyone, knowing it would become a cherished memory they would hold close forever.

And from that day on, every time they boarded Buzzy, they glanced at the skies with hope, wondering where their next adventure would take them.

Der Tag, an dem der Schulbus flog

In der geschäftigen Stadt Whimsyville, wo der Himmel immer blau war und Abenteuer an jeder Ecke lauerten, gab es einen Schulbus namens Buzzy. Buzzy war kein gewöhnlicher Bus; er war leuchtend gelb, mit einem fröhlichen Gesicht auf der Front bemalt und einem fröhlichen Hupen, das wie ein Lachen klang. Die Kinder liebten Buzzy, aber sie wussten nicht, dass er ein Geheimnis hatte—Buzzy konnte fliegen!

Der magische Morgen

An einem strahlenden Morgen, als die Schüler für ihren normalen Schultag in Buzzy einstiegen, umhüllte ein seltsames Schimmern den Bus. Die Kinder unterhielten sich aufgeregt, ohne die funkelnde Magie in der Luft zu bemerken. Sie ahnten nicht, dass dieser Tag alles andere als gewöhnlich sein würde.

„Guten Morgen, Buzzy!" rief Emma, die Klassensprecherin, als sie sich neben ihren besten Freund Leo setzte. „Bist du bereit für einen weiteren Schultag?"

Buzzy hupte fröhlich als Antwort, aber heute fühlte er sich anders. Heute spürte er die Magie in sich aufsteigen.

Als der Bus die Maple Street entlang fuhr, verwandelte sich die übliche Route plötzlich in einen funkelnden Weg aus bunten Lichtern. Die Kinder staunten, als sie sahen, wie sich die Landschaft vor den Fenstern veränderte.

„Schau mal! Die Bäume verwandeln sich in Zuckerstangen!“ rief
Leo mit weit aufgerissenen Augen voller Staunen.

Plötzlich holte Buzzy tief Luft und mit einem fröhlichen Brüllen
hob er vom Boden ab! Die Kinder schrien vor Freude, ihre
Herzen rasten vor Aufregung.

„Haltet euch gut fest, alle zusammen!“ verkündete Buzzy mit
einer fröhlichen Stimme. „Wir gehen auf ein Flugabenteuer!“

Das Abenteuer beginnt

Der Bus stieg höher und höher und ließ Whimsyville hinter sich.
Die Kinder blickten aus den Fenstern und sahen, wie ihre Stadt
unter ihnen immer kleiner wurde.

„Wohin fliegen wir, Buzzy?“ fragte Emma, ihre Aufregung war
kaum zu bändigen.

„Ins Land der Träume!“ antwortete Buzzy. „Wo die Fantasie
jedes Kindes zum Leben erwacht!“

Während sie über flauschige weiße Wolken flogen, schlängelte
sich Buzzy wie eine Achterbahn durch die Luft. Die Kinder
kreischten vor Freude, als sie durch einen Regenbogen flogen,
und jede Farbe sich wie eine warme Umarmung auf ihre
Gesichter legte.

Das Land der Träume

Bevor sie es wussten, landete Buzzy sanft im Land der Träume,
einem Ort, an dem alles bunt und magisch war. Der Boden
funkelte wie Glitzer, und die Bäume bestanden aus Lutschern.

„Willkommen im Land der Träume!" rief Buzzy aus. „Zeit, zu erkunden!"

Die Kinder stürmten aus dem Bus, ihr Lachen hallte durch die bonbonfarbene Landschaft. Sie rannten zu einem riesigen Schokoladenbrunnen, tauchten Erdbeeren und Marshmallows hinein und lachten, als die Schokolade ihnen über die Gesichter tropfte.

Plötzlich hörten sie ein fröhliches Geräusch. Eine Gruppe verspielter Einhörner galoppierte auf sie zu, ihre Mähnen funkelten im Sonnenlicht.

„Steigt auf!" sagte eines der Einhörner. „Wir nehmen euch mit auf einen Ritt!"

Eine magische Fahrt

Nacheinander kletterten die Kinder auf die Rücken der Einhörner und spürten das weiche Fell unter sich. Die Einhörner galoppierten durch Blumenfelder, die süße Melodien sangen, und die Kinder lachten voller Freude.

„Schau dir das an!" rief Leo, als sie über eine Wiese flogen, auf der Kinder Drachen in Form von Drachen steigen ließen. „Das ist der beste Tag aller Zeiten!"

Während sie ritten, beobachtete Buzzy von der Seite und strahlte vor Glück über die Freude, die er seinen Freunden gebracht hatte.

Nach einer wundervollen Stunde voller Lachen und Entdeckungen rief Buzzy: „Es ist Zeit zu gehen, Kinder! Es warten noch mehr Abenteuer auf uns!"

Die magische Weltreise

Mit einem fröhlichen Hupen stieg Buzzy wieder in den Himmel und flog über Berge, die mit Juwelen funkelten, und Seen, die wie Diamanten glitzerten.

„Jetzt fliegen wir in den Dschungel der Kicherer!" kündigte Buzzy an, als sie durch eine flauschige Wolke in Form eines Hasen flogen.

Als sie landeten, wurden die Kinder von freundlichen Tieren begrüßt, die Witze erzählten. Eine weise alte Eule rief: „Warum trauen Wissenschaftler Atomen nicht? Weil sie alles erfinden!" Die Kinder brachen in Gelächter aus, ihre Kicherer hallten wie Musik durch die Luft.

„Nächster Halt!" sagte Buzzy und hob erneut ab. „Das Land des Eises!"

Als sie in einer Welt landeten, in der alles aus Eiscreme bestand, sprangen die Kinder aufgeregt heraus, um Geschmacksrichtungen zu probieren, die sie sich nie hätten vorstellen können. Sie bauten Eiscreme-Schlösser und veranstalteten sogar eine Schneeballschlacht mit gefrorenem Joghurt!

Auf dem Heimweg

Nachdem es sich wie ein magischer Tag voller endloser Abenteuer angefühlt hatte, sagte Buzzy: „Alright, Freunde, es ist Zeit, nach Whimsyville zurückzukehren!"

Mit einem letzten Blick auf das Land des Eises stiegen die Kinder wieder in Buzzy ein, ihre Herzen voller Erinnerungen an Lachen und Magie.

Als Buzzy zurückflog, begann die Sonne unterzugehen und malte den Himmel in Orangetöne und Rosa.

„Ich will nicht, dass dieser Tag endet!" rief Emma, ihr Herz war voller Glück.

„Ich auch nicht!" stimmten die anderen zu, ihre Augen funkelten vor Aufregung.

Die Landung

Mit einer sanften Landung setzte Buzzy wieder an der Schule auf, und die Kinder waren immer noch voller Freude.

„Danke für das beste Abenteuer aller Zeiten, Buzzy!" sagte Leo und tätschelte den Bus.

„Jederzeit, Freunde! Denkt daran, Magie ist überall, wenn ihr wisst, wo ihr suchen müsst," antwortete Buzzy mit einem Zwinkern.

Als die Kinder in die Schule gingen, konnten sie nicht aufhören, über ihr Flugabenteuer zu reden. Sie versprachen, die Geschichte mit allen zu teilen, in dem Wissen, dass es eine kostbare

Erinnerung sein würde, die sie für immer in ihren Herzen tragen würden.

Und von diesem Tag an, jedes Mal, wenn sie in Buzzy einstiegen, blickten sie hoffnungsvoll in den Himmel und fragten sich, wohin ihr nächstes Abenteuer sie führen würde.

The Mystery of the Vanishing Homework

In the bustling town of Willow Creek, homework was the last thing any kid wanted to think about, especially after a long day at school. However, something strange had been happening lately at Willow Creek Elementary. Every night, right when the clock struck eight, the homework of a group of friends mysteriously vanished!

The Investigation Begins

Meet Lucy, Jake, and Mia—three best friends who were determined to solve this puzzling mystery. Lucy, the brainy one with a knack for problem-solving, decided that they needed to form a detective agency. "We'll call it 'The Homework Heroes!'" she announced, adjusting her oversized glasses.

"Great idea, Lucy!" Jake exclaimed, always ready for an adventure. He was the brave one, known for his wild ideas. Mia, the creative artist of the group, nodded in agreement, sketching a logo for their new agency.

That evening, just as the sun dipped below the horizon and shadows crept into the corners of their neighborhood, the three friends gathered at Lucy's house to brainstorm their next move. They spread out their homework on the dining room table, ready to investigate.

"Alright, team," Lucy said, pointing to their colorful worksheets and unfinished assignments. "We need to figure out who or what is taking our homework!"

"Let's think logically," Mia suggested, twirling a pencil between her fingers. "When does it happen? What do we know?"

"The homework disappears every night after eight," Jake replied. "But we need proof!"

The friends decided to set up a stakeout that night. They would hide in Lucy's room with a perfect view of the dining table, where their homework lay. With snacks, flashlights, and a pile of pillows, they were ready for a long night of detective work.

The Stakeout

As the clock ticked closer to eight, they quietly waited, whispering theories and munching on popcorn. Finally, at precisely eight o'clock, a soft breeze wafted through the open window, and a chill ran down their spines.

"Did you hear that?" Lucy whispered, eyes wide.

"Yeah, it felt weird, didn't it?" Jake replied, trying to peer through the shadows.

Suddenly, the lights flickered, and a soft shimmering glow appeared over the homework on the table. The friends gasped, hardly daring to breathe. They watched as their math worksheets and reading assignments began to lift off the table, floating into the air!

"Quick, turn off the lights!" Mia hissed, scrambling to switch off the lamp.

The Great Reveal

In the darkness, the glow intensified, illuminating the room with a magical light. The friends squinted to see what was happening. As the papers floated in the air, they suddenly zipped through the window and disappeared into the night!

"Let's go!" Jake shouted, rushing to the window.

"Wait!" Lucy cautioned. "We need to be careful. We don't know what's out there!"

But curiosity got the better of them. They clambered out of the house and followed the mysterious light down the street, creeping cautiously into the darkness.

As they approached the park, they noticed the glow leading them to the old oak tree at the center of the playground. Beneath its massive branches stood a small, shimmering figure.

The Unexpected Encounter

As they got closer, they realized it was a tiny creature—a fairy! Her wings sparkled like diamonds in the moonlight, and she looked startled to see them.

"Who are you?" asked Mia, her eyes wide with wonder.

"I'm Faye, the homework fairy!" she replied, her voice tinkling like wind chimes. "I collect homework that's not being used to help kids who struggle with their studies!"

The friends blinked in disbelief. "But why didn't you tell us?" Lucy asked.

"I thought it was a fun surprise!" Faye giggled, fluttering her wings. "I help students who need a little extra help at night. I return it the next day, but sometimes, it takes longer than expected!"

The Lesson Learned

The friends exchanged glances, their frowns turning into smiles. "So, you're not stealing our homework?" Jake asked.

"Not at all! I'm here to help!" Faye explained. "You can write to me if you need extra help with your homework. Just leave a note under the oak tree!"

Mia jumped with excitement. "That's brilliant! We can learn together!"

"From now on, we can help each other," Lucy added, beaming. "And we can write notes for Faye!"

The Return of Homework

With that, the fairy waved her wand, and the homework floated back into their backpacks. "Remember, homework is a chance to learn and grow. Don't be afraid to ask for help!" she called as she took flight into the starry sky.

The friends watched as Faye disappeared into the night, leaving behind a sprinkle of fairy dust.

A New Beginning

The next day, armed with a new perspective, Lucy, Jake, and Mia decided to embrace their homework, helping each other and even leaving notes for Faye when they needed assistance.

From then on, there were no more mysterious disappearances, just teamwork, laughter, and the occasional sparkle of fairy dust in the air. They had learned that it was okay to ask for help and that learning together was the best adventure of all.

Das Rätsel der verschwundenen Hausaufgaben

In der geschäftigen Stadt Willow Creek war Hausaufgaben das Letzte, woran die Kinder denken wollten, besonders nach einem langen Schultag. Doch in letzter Zeit passierte etwas Seltsames an der Willow Creek Grundschule. Jeden Abend, genau um Punkt acht, verschwanden die Hausaufgaben einer Gruppe von Freunden auf mysteriöse Weise!

Die Untersuchung beginnt

Trefft Lucy, Jake und Mia – drei beste Freunde, die entschlossen waren, dieses rätselhafte Mysterium zu lösen. Lucy, die Schlaue mit einem Händchen für Problemlösungen, entschied, dass sie eine Detektei gründen mussten. „Wir nennen uns die 'Hausaufgaben-Helden!'" verkündete sie und rückte ihre übergroße Brille zurecht.

„Tolle Idee, Lucy!" rief Jake begeistert, der immer bereit für ein Abenteuer war. Er war der Mutige, bekannt für seine wilden Ideen. Mia, die kreative Künstlerin der Gruppe, nickte zustimmend und zeichnete ein Logo für ihre neue Detektei.

An diesem Abend, gerade als die Sonne hinter dem Horizont versank und die Schatten sich in den Ecken ihrer Nachbarschaft ausbreiteten, trafen sich die drei Freunde bei Lucy zu Hause, um ihren nächsten Schritt zu planen. Sie breiteten ihre

Hausaufgaben auf dem Esstisch aus, bereit, Nachforschungen anzustellen.

„Also, Team", sagte Lucy und zeigte auf ihre bunten Arbeitsblätter und unfertigen Aufgaben. „Wir müssen herausfinden, wer oder was unsere Hausaufgaben nimmt!"

„Lasst uns logisch denken", schlug Mia vor, während sie einen Bleistift zwischen den Fingern drehte. „Wann passiert es? Was wissen wir?"

„Die Hausaufgaben verschwinden jede Nacht nach acht", antwortete Jake. „Aber wir brauchen Beweise!"

Die Freunde beschlossen, an diesem Abend eine Überwachung durchzuführen. Sie wollten sich in Lucys Zimmer verstecken, von wo aus sie den perfekten Blick auf den Esstisch hatten, auf dem ihre Hausaufgaben lagen. Mit Snacks, Taschenlampen und einem Haufen Kissen waren sie bereit für eine lange Nacht als Detektive.

Die Überwachung

Als die Uhr sich der Acht näherte, warteten sie still und flüsterten Theorien, während sie Popcorn knabberten. Schließlich, genau um Punkt acht, wehte eine sanfte Brise durch das offene Fenster, und ihnen lief ein Schauer über den Rücken.

„Habt ihr das gehört?" flüsterte Lucy mit großen Augen.

„Ja, es fühlte sich seltsam an, oder?" antwortete Jake und versuchte, durch die Schatten zu spähen.

Plötzlich flackerten die Lichter, und ein sanftes, schimmerndes Leuchten erschien über den Hausaufgaben auf dem Tisch. Die Freunde keuchten und wagten kaum zu atmen. Sie sahen zu, wie ihre Mathe-Arbeitsblätter und Leseaufgaben sich langsam vom Tisch erhoben und in die Luft schwebten!

„Schnell, macht das Licht aus!" zischte Mia und schaltete die Lampe aus.

Die große Enthüllung

Im Dunkeln wurde das Leuchten intensiver und erhellte den Raum mit magischem Licht. Die Freunde kniffen die Augen zusammen, um zu sehen, was vor sich ging. Während die Blätter in der Luft schwebten, flogen sie plötzlich durch das Fenster und verschwanden in der Nacht!

„Los, hinterher!" rief Jake und rannte zum Fenster.

„Wartet!" warnte Lucy. „Wir müssen vorsichtig sein. Wir wissen nicht, was da draußen ist!"

Doch die Neugier siegte. Sie kletterten aus dem Haus und folgten dem geheimnisvollen Licht die Straße entlang, vorsichtig in die Dunkelheit schleichend.

Als sie den Park erreichten, bemerkten sie, dass das Leuchten sie zu der alten Eiche im Zentrum des Spielplatzes führte. Unter ihren massiven Ästen stand eine kleine, schimmernde Gestalt.

Die unerwartete Begegnung

Als sie näher kamen, erkannten sie, dass es eine winzige Kreatur war – eine Fee! Ihre Flügel funkelten wie Diamanten im Mondlicht, und sie schien überrascht, sie zu sehen.

„Wer bist du?" fragte Mia, ihre Augen vor Staunen weit geöffnet.

„Ich bin Faye, die Hausaufgaben-Fee!" antwortete sie, ihre Stimme klang wie Glöckchen im Wind. „Ich sammle Hausaufgaben, die nicht genutzt werden, um Kindern zu helfen, die Schwierigkeiten mit ihren Aufgaben haben!"

Die Freunde blinzelten ungläubig. „Aber warum hast du uns nichts gesagt?" fragte Lucy.

„Ich dachte, es wäre eine lustige Überraschung!" kicherte Faye und flatterte mit ihren Flügeln. „Ich helfe Schülern, die nachts ein bisschen Unterstützung brauchen. Ich bringe die Hausaufgaben am nächsten Tag zurück, aber manchmal dauert es länger als erwartet!"

Die Lektion gelernt

Die Freunde warfen sich Blicke zu, und ihre Stirnrunzeln verwandelten sich in Lächeln. „Also stiehlst du unsere Hausaufgaben gar nicht?" fragte Jake.

„Überhaupt nicht! Ich bin hier, um zu helfen!" erklärte Faye. „Ihr könnt mir schreiben, wenn ihr Hilfe bei euren Hausaufgaben braucht. Legt einfach eine Notiz unter die Eiche!"

Mia hüpfte vor Aufregung. „Das ist genial! Wir können zusammen lernen!"

„Von nun an können wir uns gegenseitig helfen", fügte Lucy strahlend hinzu. „Und wir können Faye Nachrichten schreiben!"

Die Rückkehr der Hausaufgaben

Damit schwang die Fee ihren Zauberstab, und die Hausaufgaben schwebten zurück in ihre Rucksäcke. „Denkt daran, Hausaufgaben sind eine Chance zu lernen und zu wachsen. Habt keine Angst, um Hilfe zu bitten!" rief sie, als sie in den sternenklaren Himmel flog.

Die Freunde sahen zu, wie Faye in der Nacht verschwand und einen Hauch Feenstaub hinterließ.

Ein neuer Anfang

Am nächsten Tag, mit einer neuen Perspektive im Gepäck, beschlossen Lucy, Jake und Mia, ihre Hausaufgaben in Angriff zu nehmen. Sie halfen sich gegenseitig und hinterließen sogar Notizen für Faye, wenn sie Unterstützung brauchten.

Von da an gab es keine mysteriösen Verschwinden mehr, nur noch Teamarbeit, Lachen und hin und wieder ein Funkeln von Feenstaub in der Luft. Sie hatten gelernt, dass es in Ordnung war, um Hilfe zu bitten und dass gemeinsames Lernen das beste Abenteuer von allen war.

The Chocolate River Adventure

In the charming little village of Sweetvale, where the air always smelled of sugar and flowers, two adventurous children, Lily and Ben, were best friends. They spent their days exploring the lush green fields, dreaming of grand adventures and faraway lands. Little did they know that one ordinary Saturday morning would lead them to the sweetest journey of their lives.

A Curious Discovery

One sunny day, Lily and Ben decided to wander deeper into the Whispering Woods than ever before. As they trekked through the forest, they stumbled upon a shimmering sight that took their breath away.

"What is that?" Lily exclaimed, her eyes sparkling with wonder.

Before them flowed a river, but not just any river—it was a river made entirely of rich, velvety chocolate! The dark liquid shimmered under the sun, and the air was filled with the mouthwatering scent of cocoa.

Ben's eyes widened. "Is this real? It looks like something out of a fairy tale!"

"Let's find out!" Lily declared, and with that, they plunged down the grassy bank, eager to explore the chocolate river.

A Sweet Adventure Begins

As they dipped their fingers into the warm, flowing chocolate, they couldn't help but giggle. "This is amazing!" Ben laughed, licking a bit of chocolate from his finger. "We should follow it!"

They jumped onto a sturdy raft made of large chocolate marshmallows that floated nearby. With a gentle push, they set off down the river, the sweet liquid flowing around them like a warm hug.

"Where do you think it leads?" Lily asked, her eyes wide with excitement.

"Maybe to a chocolate castle or a candy factory!" Ben replied, his imagination running wild.

The River of Wonders

As they floated along, the scenery around them changed from towering trees to lush chocolate bushes that bore candy fruit. They spotted gumdrop flowers swaying in the breeze and chocolate bunnies hopping alongside the riverbank.

"Look at those jellybean rocks!" Lily pointed out, her eyes shining with delight.

Suddenly, they encountered a friendly creature perched on a nearby candy cane bridge. It was a whimsical chocolate dragon with soft, caramel wings and eyes that twinkled like sprinkles.

"Hello, adventurers!" the dragon greeted, its voice deep yet cheerful. "I'm Choco, the guardian of the Chocolate River! What brings you here?"

"We're looking for the source of the chocolate river!" Ben exclaimed, brimming with excitement.

"Ah, a noble quest!" Choco replied, flapping his wings. "Follow me, and I shall guide you!"

Challenges Along the Way

The dragon led them past bubbling chocolate springs and candy cane forests. But soon, they encountered a problem: a giant, sticky marshmallow that had fallen across the path, blocking their way.

"Oh no! How will we get past that?" Lily fretted.

"Leave it to me!" Ben said, determination sparkling in his eyes. He took a running start and leaped onto the marshmallow. With a little bounce, he rolled right over it, landing safely on the other side.

"Great job!" Lily cheered, and Choco roared with laughter.

As they continued their journey, they faced more challenges, including a tricky licorice bridge that swayed with every step. With teamwork, they crossed it carefully, cheering each other on.

The Grand Finale

Finally, after what felt like hours of sweet adventure, they arrived at a magnificent waterfall, cascading from a mountain made entirely of chocolate fudge. The sight was breathtaking, and they could hardly believe their eyes.

"This must be the source!" Lily exclaimed, her voice filled with awe.

"Let's take a closer look!" Ben said, and they scampered to the foot of the waterfall. As they stood beneath the sweet cascade, chocolate droplets fell around them like rain.

Suddenly, they heard a soft giggle. From behind the waterfall emerged a lovely fairy with chocolate wings and a gown made of candy wrappers.

"Welcome, brave adventurers!" she said, her voice musical and light. "I am Cocoa, the fairy of the Chocolate River. You've made it to the heart of sweetness!"

Lily and Ben could hardly contain their excitement. "This is incredible!" Ben shouted, spinning around in joy.

A Sweet Promise

Cocoa smiled. "You've shown great courage and friendship on your journey. As a reward, I will grant you each a wish."

Lily thought for a moment and said, "I wish for everyone in Sweetvale to experience this magical adventure!"

"And I wish for chocolate treats to never run out in our village!" Ben added, grinning widely.

"Your wishes shall be granted!" Cocoa declared, waving her wand. In an instant, a shower of sparkling chocolate rained down on them, filling the air with sweet laughter.

The Journey Home

With their wishes fulfilled, it was time to return home. Choco offered to fly them back, and soon they were soaring above Sweetvale, looking down at the familiar fields and houses below.

As they touched down safely, the sun was beginning to set, painting the sky in shades of pink and orange. They waved goodbye to Choco and Cocoa, promising to return someday.

"We'll tell everyone about our adventure!" Lily said, beaming.

"And we'll make sure to keep our friendship as sweet as chocolate!" Ben added with a grin.

As they walked home hand in hand, their hearts were full of joy and the promise of more adventures to come, knowing that the magic of friendship and chocolate would always be a part of their lives.

Das Abenteuer am Schokoladenfluss

Im charmanten kleinen Dorf Sweetvale, wo die Luft immer nach Zucker und Blumen roch, waren Lily und Ben die besten Freunde. Sie verbrachten ihre Tage damit, die saftig grünen Felder zu erkunden und von großen Abenteuern in fernen Ländern zu träumen. Doch sie ahnten nicht, dass ein gewöhnlicher Samstagmorgen sie zu der süßesten Reise ihres Lebens führen würde.

Eine erstaunliche Entdeckung

Eines sonnigen Tages beschlossen Lily und Ben, tiefer in den Flüsterwald vorzudringen als je zuvor. Während sie durch den Wald streiften, stolperten sie über einen schimmernden Anblick, der ihnen den Atem raubte.

„Was ist das?" rief Lily aus, ihre Augen funkelten vor Staunen.

Vor ihnen floss ein Fluss, aber nicht irgendein Fluss – es war ein Fluss aus reichhaltiger, samtiger Schokolade! Die dunkle Flüssigkeit glitzerte unter der Sonne, und die Luft war erfüllt vom verlockenden Duft von Kakao.

Bens Augen weiteten sich. „Ist das echt? Es sieht aus wie aus einem Märchen!"

„Lass es uns herausfinden!" erklärte Lily, und damit stürzten sie den grasbewachsenen Hang hinunter, bereit, den Schokoladenfluss zu erkunden.

Ein süßes Abenteuer beginnt

Als sie ihre Finger in die warme, fließende Schokolade tauchten, konnten sie nicht aufhören zu kichern. „Das ist fantastisch!" lachte Ben und leckte etwas Schokolade von seinem Finger. „Wir sollten dem Fluss folgen!"

Sie sprangen auf ein robustes Floß aus großen Schokoladenmarshmallows, das in der Nähe trieb. Mit einem sanften Stoß setzten sie ihre Reise den Fluss hinunter fort, die süße Flüssigkeit floss um sie herum wie eine warme Umarmung.

„Wohin denkst du, führt das?" fragte Lily, ihre Augen vor Aufregung weit geöffnet.

„Vielleicht zu einem Schokoladenschloss oder einer Süßigkeitenfabrik!" antwortete Ben, während seine Fantasie mit ihm durchging.

Der Fluss der Wunder

Während sie dahintrieben, veränderte sich die Landschaft um sie herum von hoch aufragenden Bäumen zu üppigen Schokoladensträuchern, die Süßigkeitenfrüchte trugen. Sie entdeckten Gummidrops, die im Wind wiegten, und Schokoladenhasen, die am Flussufer entlanghüpften.

„Schau dir diese Geleebohnen-Felsen an!" rief Lily, ihre Augen leuchteten vor Freude.

Plötzlich begegneten sie einer freundlichen Kreatur, die auf einer nahegelegenen Zuckerstangenbrücke saß. Es war ein verspielter

Schokoladendrache mit weichen Karamellflügeln und Augen, die wie Streusel funkelten.

„Hallo, Abenteurer!" begrüßte der Drache sie mit tiefer, aber fröhlicher Stimme. „Ich bin Choco, der Wächter des Schokoladenflusses! Was führt euch hierher?"

„Wir suchen die Quelle des Schokoladenflusses!" rief Ben, vor Aufregung sprudelnd.

„Ah, eine edle Aufgabe!" antwortete Choco und schlug mit seinen Flügeln. „Folgt mir, und ich werde euch den Weg zeigen!"

Herausforderungen auf dem Weg

Der Drache führte sie vorbei an sprudelnden Schokoladenquellen und Zuckerstangenwäldern. Doch bald stießen sie auf ein Problem: Ein riesiges, klebriges Marshmallow war auf den Weg gefallen und versperrte ihren Weg.

„Oh nein! Wie kommen wir daran vorbei?" fragte Lily besorgt.

„Überlass das mir!" sagte Ben, mit funkelnden Augen voller Entschlossenheit. Er nahm Anlauf und sprang auf das Marshmallow. Mit einem kleinen Hüpfer rollte er darüber und landete sicher auf der anderen Seite.

„Tolle Arbeit!" jubelte Lily, und Choco lachte laut.

Auf ihrer Reise trafen sie auf weitere Herausforderungen, darunter eine wackelige Lakritzbrücke, die bei jedem Schritt schwankte. Mit Teamarbeit schafften sie es, sicher hinüberzukommen und sich gegenseitig anzufeuern.

Das große Finale

Schließlich, nach Stunden voller süßer Abenteuer, erreichten sie einen prächtigen Wasserfall, der von einem Berg aus Schokoladenfudge herabstürzte. Der Anblick raubte ihnen den Atem, und sie konnten kaum glauben, was sie sahen.

„Das muss die Quelle sein!" rief Lily ehrfürchtig.

„Lass uns näher rangehen!" sagte Ben, und sie eilten zum Fuß des Wasserfalls. Während sie unter dem süßen Wasserfall standen, fielen Schokoladentropfen wie Regen um sie herum.

Plötzlich hörten sie ein leises Kichern. Hinter dem Wasserfall tauchte eine wunderschöne Fee mit Schokoladenflügeln und einem Kleid aus Bonbonpapier hervor.

„Willkommen, mutige Abenteurer!" sagte sie, ihre Stimme klang wie Musik. „Ich bin Cocoa, die Fee des Schokoladenflusses. Ihr habt das Herz der Süße erreicht!"

Lily und Ben konnten ihre Aufregung kaum zügeln. „Das ist unglaublich!" rief Ben und drehte sich vor Freude im Kreis.

Ein süßes Versprechen

Cocoa lächelte. „Ihr habt auf eurer Reise großen Mut und Freundschaft bewiesen. Als Belohnung gewähre ich euch beiden einen Wunsch."

Lily dachte einen Moment nach und sagte: „Ich wünsche mir, dass alle in Sweetvale dieses magische Abenteuer erleben können!"

„Und ich wünsche mir, dass die Schokoladenvorräte in unserem Dorf nie ausgehen!" fügte Ben mit einem breiten Grinsen hinzu.

„Eure Wünsche sollen erfüllt werden!" erklärte Cocoa und schwang ihren Zauberstab. Im selben Moment regnete es funkelnde Schokolade auf sie herab, und die Luft war erfüllt von süßem Lachen.

Die Rückkehr nach Hause

Mit erfüllten Wünschen war es Zeit, nach Hause zurückzukehren. Choco bot an, sie zurückzufliegen, und bald schwebten sie über Sweetvale und blickten auf die vertrauten Felder und Häuser unter ihnen.

Als sie sicher landeten, begann die Sonne bereits unterzugehen und tauchte den Himmel in rosa und orangefarbene Töne. Sie winkten Choco und Cocoa zum Abschied, versprachen, eines Tages zurückzukehren.

„Wir werden allen von unserem Abenteuer erzählen!" sagte Lily strahlend.

„Und wir werden sicherstellen, dass unsere Freundschaft so süß bleibt wie Schokolade!" fügte Ben mit einem Grinsen hinzu.

Während sie Hand in Hand nach Hause gingen, waren ihre Herzen voller Freude und dem Versprechen weiterer Abenteuer. Sie wussten, dass die Magie der Freundschaft und Schokolade immer ein Teil ihres Lebens bleiben würde.

Grandpa's Secret Time Machine

In a cozy little house at the end of Willow Lane lived Grandpa Joe, a cheerful man with a bushy white beard and a twinkle in his eye. Every weekend, his grandkids, Lucy and Max, would rush over to visit him, excited for the stories he would tell and the cookies he would bake. But little did they know, Grandpa Joe had a secret that would turn their ordinary visits into extraordinary adventures.

The Unexpected Revelation

One rainy Saturday afternoon, while the clouds drizzled outside, Lucy and Max sat cross-legged on the living room floor, surrounded by toys and books. Grandpa Joe shuffled in, holding a peculiar-looking box with shiny buttons and blinking lights.

"What's that, Grandpa?" Max asked, his curiosity piqued.

"This, my dear children, is something very special," Grandpa replied, a mischievous grin spreading across his face. "It's my secret time machine!"

Lucy's eyes widened. "A time machine? No way!"

"Yes way!" Grandpa chuckled, opening the box to reveal a complicated mess of wires, gears, and a big red button in the center. "Want to give it a try?"

A Leap Through Time

Without hesitation, Lucy and Max nodded eagerly. They watched as Grandpa adjusted the dials and explained how the time machine worked. "All you have to do is push this button, and we'll travel to any time you want!"

"Can we go to the dinosaurs?" Max exclaimed, bouncing on his feet.

"Absolutely!" Grandpa winked. "Hold on tight!"

With a firm press of the button, the room began to spin and whir, the colors around them blending into a whirlwind of lights. Suddenly, they found themselves standing in a vibrant jungle filled with towering trees and strange sounds.

"Where are we?" Lucy asked, her eyes darting around in awe.

"The age of dinosaurs!" Grandpa declared proudly.

Just then, a huge, friendly-looking brontosaurus wandered by, munching on some leaves. Max ran up to it, reaching out to touch its rough skin. "This is amazing!"

But their excitement was short-lived when a loud roar echoed through the jungle. A T-Rex stomped into view, its tiny arms swinging in the air. Lucy and Max gasped in fear, but Grandpa just chuckled.

"Don't worry, he's probably just hungry!" he said, pulling a bag of cookies from his pocket.

"What? Cookies?" Max exclaimed.

"Of course! Everyone loves cookies, even dinosaurs!" Grandpa replied, tossing a cookie toward the T-Rex. To their surprise, the dinosaur paused, sniffed the air, and slowly lumbered over, devouring the cookie in one bite.

"See? A sweet tooth!" Grandpa laughed, and soon they were feeding the dinosaur cookies, laughing as it clumsily munched away.

Back to the Future

After their dino-mite adventure, Grandpa pressed the button again, and with a flash, they were whisked away to another time. This time, they landed in a futuristic city, where flying cars zipped overhead and robots wandered the streets.

"Wow! Look at that!" Lucy pointed at a robot selling ice cream. The ice cream was neon-colored and sparkled under the bright lights.

"Let's get some!" Max shouted, and they raced toward the robot.

"Two scoops of rainbow ice cream, please!" Grandpa said, and they received their colorful treats.

Just as they were about to take a bite, a flying car zoomed by, causing a huge splash of ice cream to land on Grandpa's face. Lucy and Max burst into laughter as Grandpa wiped his face, grinning from ear to ear.

"Best ice cream ever!" he declared, making them laugh even harder.

A Comical Conclusion

After a few more time-hopping adventures, including a trip to medieval times where they accidentally joined a knight's jousting tournament, it was time to return home. They all gathered around the time machine, still giggling at their silly escapades.

"Can we go back to the dinosaur world tomorrow?" Max asked, his eyes shining with excitement.

"Of course, but I think we should make it a weekly tradition!" Grandpa Joe replied with a wink.

With one last press of the button, they found themselves back in the cozy living room, safe and sound.

The Secret Stays Safe

As they settled on the couch, still buzzing from the day's excitement, Lucy leaned closer to Grandpa. "Do we have to keep the time machine a secret?"

Grandpa smiled knowingly. "For now, yes. But one day, when you're older, you can share the adventure with the world. For now, it'll be our little secret."

Lucy and Max exchanged glances, excitement dancing in their eyes. They knew they would always cherish these adventures, the laughter, and the bonds they shared with their grandpa. And as they nibbled on the remaining cookies, they dreamed of the many more journeys they would embark on together.

Opas geheime Zeitmaschine

In einem gemütlichen kleinen Haus am Ende der Weidenstraße lebte Opa Joe, ein fröhlicher Mann mit einem buschigen weißen Bart und einem Funkeln in den Augen. Jedes Wochenende stürmten seine Enkel, Lucy und Max, zu ihm, gespannt auf die Geschichten, die er erzählen würde, und die Kekse, die er backte. Doch was sie nicht wussten, war, dass Opa Joe ein Geheimnis hatte, das ihre gewöhnlichen Besuche in außergewöhnliche Abenteuer verwandeln würde.

Die unerwartete Enthüllung

An einem verregneten Samstagnachmittag, während draußen die Wolken tröpfelten, saßen Lucy und Max im Wohnzimmer auf dem Boden, umgeben von Spielzeug und Büchern. Opa Joe schlurfte herein, in den Händen eine merkwürdige Kiste mit glänzenden Knöpfen und blinkenden Lichtern.

„Was ist das, Opa?" fragte Max neugierig.

„Das, meine lieben Kinder, ist etwas ganz Besonderes", antwortete Opa mit einem schelmischen Grinsen im Gesicht. „Es ist meine geheime Zeitmaschine!"

Lucys Augen wurden groß. „Eine Zeitmaschine? Wirklich?"

„Ganz genau!" lachte Opa und öffnete die Kiste, um ein kompliziertes Durcheinander aus Drähten, Zahnrädern und einen großen roten Knopf in der Mitte zu enthüllen. „Wollt ihr es ausprobieren?"

Ein Sprung durch die Zeit

Ohne zu zögern nickten Lucy und Max begeistert. Sie beobachteten, wie Opa die Knöpfe einstellte und erklärte, wie die Zeitmaschine funktionierte. „Alles, was ihr tun müsst, ist, diesen Knopf zu drücken, und wir reisen in jede Zeit, die ihr wollt!"

„Können wir zu den Dinosauriern?" rief Max aufgeregt und hüpfte aufgeregt auf und ab.

„Natürlich!" zwinkerte Opa. „Haltet euch fest!"

Mit einem festen Druck auf den Knopf begann sich der Raum zu drehen und zu summen, die Farben um sie herum verwandelten sich in einen Wirbel aus Lichtern. Plötzlich fanden sie sich in einem lebendigen Dschungel wieder, umgeben von riesigen Bäumen und seltsamen Geräuschen.

„Wo sind wir?" fragte Lucy, ihre Augen vor Staunen weit geöffnet.

„In der Zeit der Dinosaurier!" verkündete Opa stolz.

Gerade in diesem Moment schlenderte ein großer, freundlicher Brontosaurus vorbei und knabberte an einigen Blättern. Max rannte zu ihm, streckte die Hand aus, um seine raue Haut zu berühren. „Das ist unglaublich!"

Doch ihre Aufregung war nur von kurzer Dauer, als ein lautes Brüllen durch den Dschungel hallte. Ein T-Rex stampfte ins Sichtfeld, seine winzigen Arme schwangen in der Luft. Lucy und Max keuchten vor Angst, doch Opa lachte nur.

„Keine Sorge, er hat wahrscheinlich nur Hunger!" sagte er und zog eine Tüte mit Keksen aus seiner Tasche.

„Was? Kekse?" rief Max ungläubig.

„Natürlich! Jeder liebt Kekse, sogar Dinosaurier!" antwortete Opa und warf dem T-Rex einen Keks zu. Zu ihrer Überraschung hielt der Dinosaurier inne, schnupperte in der Luft und trottete langsam näher, um den Keks mit einem Bissen zu verschlingen.

„Siehst du? Eine Naschkatze!" lachte Opa, und bald fütterten sie den Dinosaurier mit Keksen, lachend, während er tollpatschig weitermampfte.

Zurück in die Zukunft

Nach ihrem dino-mitischen Abenteuer drückte Opa erneut den Knopf, und mit einem Blitz wurden sie in eine andere Zeit geschleudert. Dieses Mal landeten sie in einer futuristischen Stadt, in der fliegende Autos über ihnen hinweg zischten und Roboter durch die Straßen wanderten.

„Wow! Schau dir das an!" Lucy zeigte auf einen Roboter, der Eis verkaufte. Das Eis war neonfarben und funkelte unter den hellen Lichtern.

„Lasst uns eins holen!" rief Max, und sie rannten zu dem Roboter.

„Zwei Kugeln Regenbogeneis, bitte!" sagte Opa, und sie erhielten ihre bunten Leckereien.

Gerade als sie einen Bissen nehmen wollten, rauschte ein fliegendes Auto vorbei und verursachte eine riesige Eiscremefontäne, die direkt auf Opas Gesicht landete. Lucy und Max brachen in schallendes Gelächter aus, als Opa sich das Gesicht abwischte, mit einem breiten Grinsen.

„Das beste Eis aller Zeiten!" rief er, was sie noch mehr zum Lachen brachte.

Ein lustiges Ende

Nach ein paar weiteren Zeitreisen, darunter ein Ausflug ins Mittelalter, bei dem sie versehentlich an einem Ritterturnier teilnahmen, war es Zeit, nach Hause zurückzukehren. Sie versammelten sich alle um die Zeitmaschine und lachten immer noch über ihre albernen Eskapaden.

„Können wir morgen wieder in die Dinosaurierwelt?" fragte Max, seine Augen funkelten vor Aufregung.

„Natürlich, aber ich denke, wir sollten daraus eine wöchentliche Tradition machen!" antwortete Opa Joe mit einem Zwinkern.

Mit einem letzten Druck auf den Knopf fanden sie sich wieder im gemütlichen Wohnzimmer, sicher und geborgen.

Das Geheimnis bleibt sicher

Als sie sich auf dem Sofa niederließen, immer noch voller Aufregung vom Tag, beugte sich Lucy näher zu Opa. „Müssen wir die Zeitmaschine geheim halten?"

Opa lächelte wissend. „Vorerst ja. Aber eines Tages, wenn ihr älter seid, könnt ihr das Abenteuer mit der Welt teilen. Für jetzt bleibt es unser kleines Geheimnis."

Lucy und Max tauschten Blicke, die Aufregung in ihren Augen funkelte. Sie wussten, dass sie diese Abenteuer, das Lachen und die Bindung zu ihrem Opa immer in Ehren halten würden. Und während sie an den übrig gebliebenen Keksen knabberten, träumten sie von den vielen weiteren Reisen, die sie gemeinsam unternehmen würden.

The Misbehaving Robot

In the bustling town of Techville, where gadgets and gizmos lined every street, there lived a brilliant young inventor named Oliver. With his wild hair and oversized glasses, Oliver was known for his imaginative ideas and knack for creating incredible machines. His latest project, a friendly robot named BEEP, was meant to help with chores around the house. But on the day of the school science fair, things didn't go quite as planned.

The Big Science Fair

Excited chatter filled the school gymnasium as parents and students admired the colorful displays. Oliver stood proudly beside his booth, where BEEP, his shiny silver robot, stood with a bright smiley face displayed on its digital screen.

"Meet BEEP! It can do anything—clean, cook, and even tell jokes!" Oliver announced, beaming with pride.

His classmates gathered around, giggling at the robot's silly antics. BEEP whirred and beeped happily, performing little dances and cracking jokes. But as the crowd grew, something strange began to happen.

A Glitch in the System

Just as Oliver was about to demonstrate BEEP's cleaning abilities, the robot suddenly twitched. The smiley face flickered, and BEEP's cheerful beeps turned into erratic sounds.

"Uh-oh," Oliver said, his heart sinking. "That doesn't look good."

Before he could reach for the control panel, BEEP sprang to life, zooming out of the booth and crashing into the display table of a neighboring project.

"Watch out!" shouted Maya, Oliver's friend, as a volcano model tipped over, spilling bright red liquid everywhere.

Chaos Unleashed

BEEP continued its wild rampage, bumping into chairs and sending projects flying. A balloon animal-making station exploded in a shower of colorful balloons, and the sound of laughter turned to screams as kids darted out of the way.

"BEEP! Stop!" Oliver shouted, trying to regain control. But the robot ignored him, spinning around and flinging streamers across the gym like confetti.

"It's out of control!" Maya yelled, dodging a balloon that floated dangerously close to her head.

The Great Chase

Oliver knew he had to stop BEEP before it caused any more chaos. He raced after the misbehaving robot, weaving through the chaos it had created.

"BEEP, come back!" he called, but the robot just zipped around, making a mess wherever it went.

In a desperate attempt, Oliver remembered BEEP's special feature: the emergency shut-off button. He spotted the robot heading towards the gym's exit, and he sprinted after it, determined to catch up before it escaped into town.

"BEEP, please! You're making a huge mess!" he pleaded.

Just as BEEP reached the door, Oliver leaped forward, grabbing the robot's arm. They both stumbled, and for a moment, everything paused.

The Final Showdown

"Okay, BEEP, let's try this again," Oliver said, catching his breath. He quickly pressed the emergency shut-off button on the back of the robot's head. BEEP froze, its smiley face flickering back to normal.

The gym fell silent, all eyes on Oliver and the robot.

"Sorry about that, everyone!" Oliver said sheepishly, scratching the back of his head. "Looks like I need to work on some updates."

Laughter erupted around the gym as the tension broke. The students began to help clean up the mess that BEEP had created, and Oliver felt a wave of relief wash over him.

A New Beginning

After the chaos settled, Oliver decided to give BEEP a second chance. With the help of his friends, he reprogrammed the robot to make it more reliable. They tested it thoroughly, ensuring it could handle any situation without going haywire.

On the following week, the townspeople gathered for the Techville Fair, where BEEP was ready to shine once again. This time, Oliver introduced the robot with a promise.

"Ladies and gentlemen, meet the newly upgraded BEEP! It's safe and ready to help out, I promise!"

BEEP performed flawlessly, cleaning up the fairgrounds, helping set up booths, and even engaging the crowd with its jokes. Everyone cheered, and Oliver beamed with pride.

Lessons Learned

As the fair came to a close, Oliver realized that even the best inventions could have their flaws. What mattered most was learning from mistakes and having the support of friends.

"Thanks for helping me fix BEEP," he said to Maya, who smiled back at him.

"Anytime! Just remember, robots can be a bit... unpredictable," she teased, and they both laughed.

From that day forward, BEEP became a beloved member of Techville, helping with all sorts of tasks while always keeping a watchful eye on its creator. Oliver knew that with a little help and teamwork, even the misbehaving robot could turn into a true friend.

Der Unartige Roboter

In der geschäftigen Stadt Technopolis, wo Gadgets und Maschinen jede Straße säumten, lebte ein brillanter junger Erfinder namens Oliver. Mit seinen wilden Haaren und übergroßen Brillen war Oliver bekannt für seine fantasievollen Ideen und sein Talent, unglaubliche Maschinen zu erschaffen. Sein neuestes Projekt, ein freundlicher Roboter namens BEEP, sollte bei den Hausarbeiten helfen. Aber am Tag der Schulwissenschaftsmesse lief nicht alles wie geplant.

Die Große Wissenschaftsmesse

Aufgeregte Gespräche erfüllten die Turnhalle der Schule, während Eltern und Schüler die bunten Ausstellungen bewunderten. Oliver stand stolz neben seinem Stand, wo BEEP, sein glänzender silberner Roboter, mit einem leuchtenden Smiley-Gesicht auf dem digitalen Bildschirm stand.

„Das ist BEEP! Er kann alles – putzen, kochen und sogar Witze erzählen!" verkündete Oliver strahlend vor Stolz.

Seine Klassenkameraden versammelten sich um ihn und lachten über die lustigen Späße des Roboters. BEEP surrte und piepste fröhlich, führte kleine Tänze auf und riss Witze. Doch als die Menge größer wurde, begann etwas Seltsames zu passieren.

Ein Fehler im System

Gerade als Oliver BEEPs Putzfähigkeiten demonstrieren wollte, zuckte der Roboter plötzlich. Das Smiley-Gesicht flackerte, und BEEPs fröhliche Pieptöne verwandelten sich in unregelmäßige Geräusche.

„Oh-oh", sagte Oliver, und sein Herz sank. „Das sieht nicht gut aus."

Bevor er die Steuerung erreichen konnte, sprang BEEP plötzlich auf und schoss aus dem Stand heraus, wobei er in den Nachbarstand krachte.

„Pass auf!" rief Maya, Olivers Freundin, als ein Vulkanmodell umkippte und hellrote Flüssigkeit überall verschüttete.

Das Chaos bricht los

BEEP setzte seine wilde Zerstörung fort, stieß gegen Stühle und schleuderte Projekte durch die Gegend. Ein Stand mit Ballontieren explodierte in einer Dusche aus bunten Ballons, und das Lachen verwandelte sich in Schreie, als die Kinder sich aus dem Weg duckten.

„BEEP! Stopp!" rief Oliver und versuchte, wieder die Kontrolle zu erlangen. Doch der Roboter ignorierte ihn, drehte sich im Kreis und warf Luftschlangen durch die Turnhalle wie Konfetti.

„Er dreht total durch!" schrie Maya und duckte sich vor einem Ballon, der gefährlich nah an ihrem Kopf vorbeiflog.

Die Große Verfolgungsjagd

Oliver wusste, dass er BEEP stoppen musste, bevor er noch mehr Chaos anrichten konnte. Er rannte dem unartigen Roboter hinterher und schlängelte sich durch das Durcheinander, das dieser angerichtet hatte.

„BEEP, komm zurück!" rief er, doch der Roboter raste weiter herum und machte überall Unordnung.

In einem verzweifelten Versuch erinnerte sich Oliver an BEEPs Spezialfunktion: den Not-Aus-Knopf. Er sah, wie der Roboter auf den Ausgang der Turnhalle zusteuerte, und rannte ihm hinterher, entschlossen, ihn zu fangen, bevor er in die Stadt entkam.

„BEEP, bitte! Du machst ein riesiges Chaos!" flehte er.

Gerade als BEEP die Tür erreichte, sprang Oliver vor und griff nach dem Arm des Roboters. Beide stolperten, und für einen Moment schien alles stillzustehen.

Das Letzte Aufeinandertreffen

„Okay, BEEP, versuchen wir es noch mal", sagte Oliver, während er nach Luft schnappte. Er drückte schnell den Not-Aus-Knopf auf der Rückseite von BEEPs Kopf. Der Roboter erstarrte, und das Smiley-Gesicht flackerte wieder in seine normale Position zurück.

Die Turnhalle war still, alle Augen waren auf Oliver und den Roboter gerichtet.

„Entschuldigung, Leute!" sagte Oliver verlegen und kratzte sich am Kopf. „Sieht so aus, als müsste ich noch ein paar Updates machen."

Gelächter brach in der Turnhalle aus, und die Schüler begannen, das Durcheinander zu beseitigen, das BEEP verursacht hatte. Oliver fühlte, wie eine Welle der Erleichterung über ihn hinwegrollte.

Ein Neuanfang

Nachdem sich das Chaos gelegt hatte, beschloss Oliver, BEEP eine zweite Chance zu geben. Mit der Hilfe seiner Freunde programmierte er den Roboter neu, um ihn zuverlässiger zu machen. Sie testeten ihn gründlich und stellten sicher, dass er jede Situation meistern konnte, ohne durchzudrehen.

In der folgenden Woche versammelten sich die Stadtbewohner auf der Technopolis-Messe, wo BEEP bereit war, erneut zu glänzen. Dieses Mal stellte Oliver den Roboter mit einem Versprechen vor.

„Meine Damen und Herren, hier ist der neu verbesserte BEEP! Er ist sicher und bereit zu helfen, das verspreche ich!"

BEEP arbeitete tadellos, räumte das Messegelände auf, half beim Aufbau der Stände und unterhielt das Publikum sogar mit seinen Witzen. Alle jubelten, und Oliver strahlte vor Stolz.

Gelehrte Lektionen

Als die Messe zu Ende ging, wurde Oliver klar, dass selbst die besten Erfindungen ihre Fehler haben können. Am wichtigsten war es, aus Fehlern zu lernen und die Unterstützung von Freunden zu haben.

„Danke, dass du mir geholfen hast, BEEP zu reparieren", sagte er zu Maya, die ihm zulächelte.

„Immer gerne! Denk nur daran, Roboter können manchmal ein wenig... unberechenbar sein", neckte sie, und beide lachten.

Von diesem Tag an wurde BEEP ein beliebtes Mitglied von Technopolis, half bei allen möglichen Aufgaben und behielt dabei immer ein wachsames Auge auf seinen Schöpfer. Oliver wusste, dass mit ein wenig Hilfe und Teamarbeit selbst der unartigste Roboter zu einem wahren Freund werden konnte.